Contents

Animals can be superheroes!

Have you ever wanted to be a superhero and help others using your superpowers? Did you know that both wild animals and pets have used their skills to look after others? Read this book to find out which animal helpers have come to the rescue by using their super skills.

Some animals have been helpers in times of danger.

Super rescue

Dolphins can sense when people are in danger. In 2004, a family was swimming in New Zealand when a great white shark swam at them. Suddenly, about six dolphins formed a barrier around them to keep the shark away. When the shark gave up, the dolphins helped the swimmers back to shore.

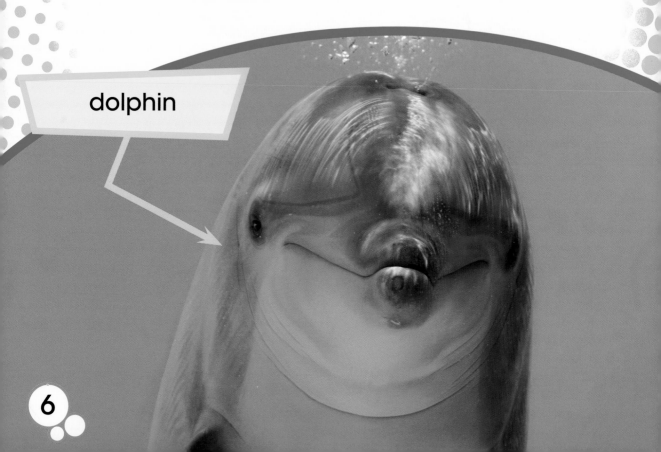

dolphin

great white shark

Super friend

Seals are clever sea **mammals** with amazing skills. In 2002, a dog swimming in the River Tees was swept away downriver. Suddenly, a seal's head popped up and circled the drowning dog. Then the seal nudged the dog with its nose to push it to shore. Safe at last!

Super warning

Elephants can pick up sounds and **vibrations** in the ground through their feet and trunks. When a **tsunami** struck Thailand in 2004, elephants seemed to know it was coming. Many moved to higher ground to escape and took their tourist riders with them.

Did you know?
Elephants helped to clear up the damage caused by the tsunami.

Super insects

Ants are mini superheroes. For their size, they are super-strong and can lift 20 times their own body weight. That is not all. Some ants act like heroes to save each other from a **predator**, even when they risk getting killed themselves.

Ants work as a team to build a bridge, so other ants can crawl over the gap.

Did you know?

If food is too big to carry back to the nest, the ant fetches another ant to help it carry the food.

Super caring

Although gorillas can be **aggressive**, they can act like superheroes. In 1996, a gorilla called Binti Jua helped a three-year-old boy when he fell into her pen. She rushed over to comfort him. She kept him safe from other gorillas until he could be rescued.

Super saver

Whales can be super-intelligent and caring. Mila, a beluga whale, stopped a diver from drowning in China in 2009. Yang Yun dived to the bottom of Mila's pool in "Polar Land". But bad **cramps** stopped her returning to the surface. Mila rushed to the rescue, grabbed Yun's leg, and pushed her up to get air.

Yang Yun

Mila

17

Super flight

Pigeons have been used to carry messages because of their skill in flying long distances and finding their way. In fog at sea in World War 2, the crew of a crashed plane sent pigeons with details of where they were. After rescue came, the pigeons received the **Dickin Medal** for animal bravery.

message

Did you know?

In wars, carrier pigeons saved lives by carrying important secret messages through gunfire.

Super pet

Cats are not just clever, they also have super **vision** and hearing. One night in 2010, in his New Zealand home, Maceo the cat sensed danger. A neighbour's shed was on fire. Maceo dipped his paws into the toilet then walked over his owners' faces. They woke to escape, just in time.

Maceo's owners woke to see a blaze right outside their window.

Super cool

Some horses can be super-brave. During World War 2, police horses received medals for being heroes. In 1947, when bombs fell on London, a window smashed down in front of police horse Olga. She bolted in fear but returned to the scene to help with rescues.

Olga

Super sniffer

As man's best friend, dogs are our most **loyal** animal superhero helpers. Their excellent hearing, sense of smell, and super-intelligence make many dogs real heroes during danger. Two dogs awarded medals for bravery were Endal and Treo.

Endal was voted "Dog of the Millennium" and received a "Golden Bone" award for his work with his disabled owner.

Treo was awarded a **Dickin Medal** for sniffing out roadside bombs in Afghanistan.

Super brave

A pet dog called Angel became a hero in 2010, when he stopped a mountain lion attacking an 11-year-old boy in Canada. The boy was collecting firewood outside his home when the wild cat attacked. Angel was badly hurt, but he recovered and was praised for saving the boy's life.

Did you know?

The mountain lion is also known as a puma or cougar.

Quiz: Spot the superhero!

Test your powers of observation and see if you can spot the superhero. You can find the answers on page 32 if you are really stuck!

1. Which of these animals has saved people from sharks?
a) a dog
b) a dolphin
c) a seal

2. Which of these animals can hear through their feet?
a) an elephant
b) an ant
c) a whale

3. Which of these animals has worked for the police?
a) a horse
b) a gorilla
c) a cat

4. Which of these animals has won medals?
a) a shark
b) a pigeon
c) a puma

5. Which of these animals has rescued people?
a) a dog
b) an ant
c) a cougar

Glossary

aggressive unfriendly and likely to attack

cramps muscle pains

Dickin Medal award for bravery presented to animals in the United Kingdom

loyal faithful and reliable

mammal warm-blooded animal that makes milk for its young

predator animal that hunts other animals

tsunami great sea wave produced by an earthquake or volcano under the sea

vibration trembling movement

vision eyesight

Find out more

Books

Amazing Animal Families, Honor Head, Brenda Williams, and Brian Williams (TickTock, 2009)

Animals (Record Breakers), Daniel Gilpin (Wayland, 2010)

First Encylopedia of Animals, Paul Dowswell (Usborne, 2011)

Websites

www.bbc.co.uk/newsround/15749027
Find out about heroic horses used in battle.

**www.pdsa.org.uk/pet-protectors/read/
pet-heroes**
Find out about animal awards.

Index

Answers: 1b, 2a, 3a, 4b, 5a.